Bob Chilcott

Times and Seasons

8 SONGS FOR UPPER VOICES

MUSIC DEPARTMENT

OXFORD
UNIVERSITY PRESS

OXFORD
UNIVERSITY PRESS

Great Clarendon Street, Oxford OX2 6DP,
United Kingdom

Oxford University Press is a department of the University of Oxford.
It furthers the University's objective of excellence in research, scholarship,
and education by publishing worldwide. Oxford is a registered trade mark of
Oxford University Press in the UK and in certain other countries

© Oxford University Press 2019

Database right Oxford University Press (maker)

First published 2019

Impression: 1

ISBN 978-0-19-353088-1

Music and text origination by
Katie Johnston
Printed in Great Britain on acid-free paper by
Halstan & Co. Ltd, Amersham, Bucks.

Contents

Composer's note

This collection of songs casts the times of the day and the seasons of the year in a voice of youthful optimism. The new poems have been specially written by Delphine Chalmers, who at the time of writing is about to begin her third year as an undergraduate at the University of Oxford. Delphine's tender and elegant words suggested pairing *a cappella* folk-like melodies for the times of day with more rhapsodic, accompanied songs for the seasons of the year. The pairs of songs (a time and a season each) were written for three school choirs, from Japan, Australia, and England (Delphine's old school), and a renowned children's choir from Germany, with whom I have worked over the last few years. These pieces can be sung together as a set or separately as stand-alone songs.

for Keisuke Nakajima and the Kurume Shin-ai High School Choir, Fukuoka, Japan

Morning

Delphine Chalmers
(b. 1998)

BOB CHILCOTT
(b. 1955)

Duration: 2 mins

yes - ter - day   And   make   each   foot - step___   glit - ter,   and

make   each   foot - step___   glit - ter,   glit - ter.___

Like   a___   flower   that___   strives   to   grow   I   long   to   crane   my   neck.

Find - ing___   in   your___   warmth   the   life,   the   life   that   will   fuse   me

to   this   world   And   hold   my   quest - ing   roots___   firm,___   and

hold   my   quest - ing   roots___   firm,___   my   quest - ing   roots___

firm   And   know   I   am___   re - born,___   and

know   I   am___   re - born,___   I   am   re - born.___

for Keisuke Nakajima and the Kurume Shin-ai High School Choir, Fukuoka, Japan

Spring

Delphine Chalmers
(b. 1998)

BOB CHILCOTT
(b. 1955)

Duration: 3 mins

Lyrics (Soprano "ah"; Alto):

To-day_ is one of those days_____ When the sky roars by in a co-balt blaze,

Dom-ing far__ a - bove   our reach.   To-day_ is one of those   days_

When the   trees stretch out   their fin - gers

When I see the beau-ty of the world Gleam-ing out - ward

from with-in.__ To-day_ is one of those days_____ And I

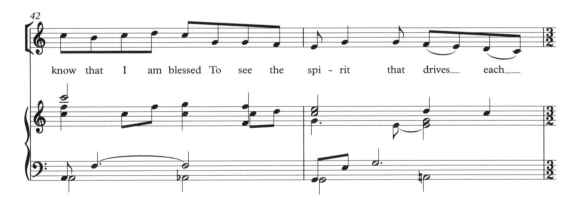

know that I am blessed To see the spi - rit that drives_ each_

liv - ing thing. So, I'll un - furl my hands, Let my

for Jenny Moon and Bel Canto, Hillcrest Christian College, Queensland, Australia

Midday

Delphine Chalmers
(b. 1998)

BOB CHILCOTT
(b. 1955)

Duration: 1.5 mins

if you ask her kind - ly She will let you see The__

snow-drop grins and li - ly tears, The for - get - me-nots of his - to -

- ry. And when the__ fi - nal se - cond lands__

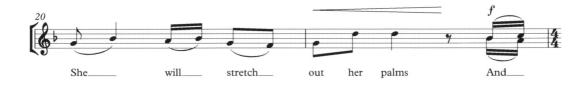

She__ will__ stretch__ out her palms And__

if you love her wise - ly She will let you take The__

fu - ture from her fin - gers:__ Your gar - den is your own to__ make.

for Jenny Moon and Bel Canto, Hillcrest Christian College, Queensland, Australia

Summer

Delphine Chalmers
(b. 1998)

BOB CHILCOTT
(b. 1955)

Duration: 2 mins

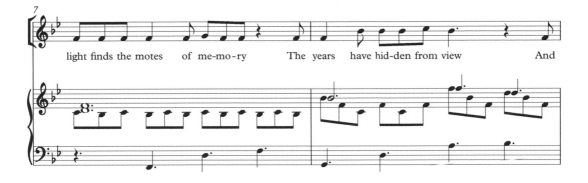

light finds the motes of me-mo-ry The years have hid-den from view And

makes me, and makes me dream___ a-gain.___ In

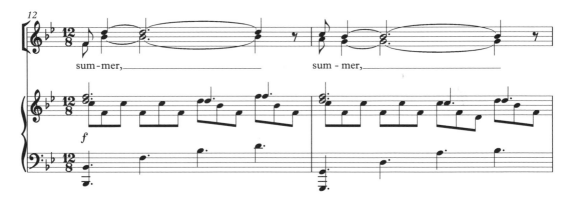

sum-mer,___ sum-mer,

sum-mer,___ sum - mer.___ You

shared my worlds and dap-pled dens, my worlds and dap - pled dens, The

first stings that taught me how to feel._____ With

fruit - bruised lips and sun - brown legs I chased with length'n - ing strides The

sha - dow of who I might___ be-come.___ In

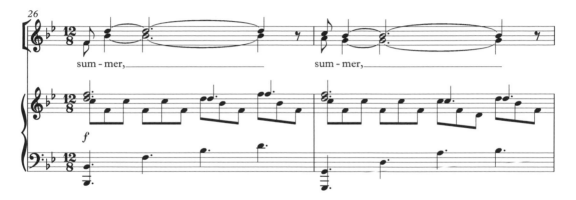

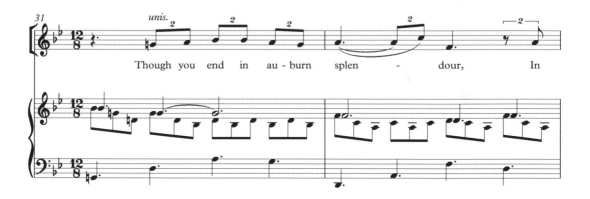

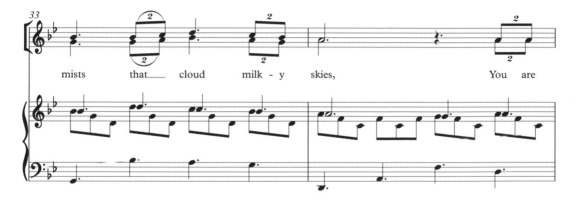

al - ways__ there for me in whis - pers,   in

whis - pers,   whis - pers.   ah_____   ah

whis - pers,   whis - pers.   ah_____   ah_____

__ ah_____   ah_____

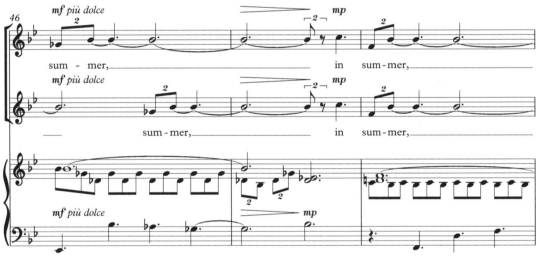

for Stephen Willis and the choir of The Abbey School, Reading

Evening

Delphine Chalmers
(b. 1998)

BOB CHILCOTT
(b. 1955)

Duration: 2 mins

for Stephen Willis and the choir of The Abbey School, Reading

Autumn

Delphine Chalmers
(b. 1998)

BOB CHILCOTT
(b. 1955)

au - tumn light has a Mi - das touch, A gold - en blush that gives our world a

gift. Her ear - rings are pearls of snail shell, Her

Duration: 2 mins

neck is_ draped in horse - chest - nut beads, Her

hands_ gleam with ru - by rings Just for you and me But

what, what can we of - fer?_ The

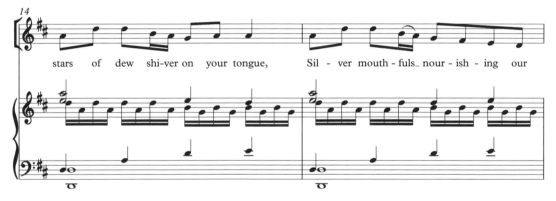

stars of dew shi-ver on your tongue, Sil - ver mouth-fuls_ nour-ish-ing our

world.   Her   mists   are — steam   on a   la - den   spoon,   Her

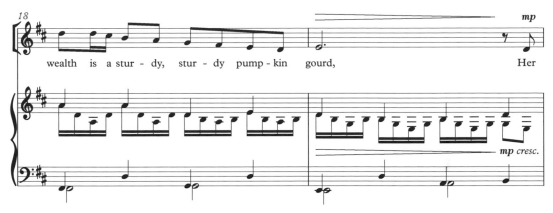

wealth   is   a   stur - dy,   stur - dy   pump - kin   gourd,   Her

mes - sage   is   a   self - less   love   Just   for   you   and   me   But   what,   what can we

of - fer? —

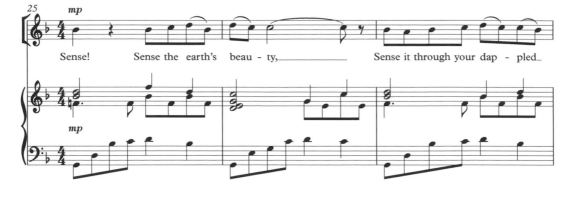

Sense! Sense the earth's beau-ty,_____ Sense it through your dap - pled_

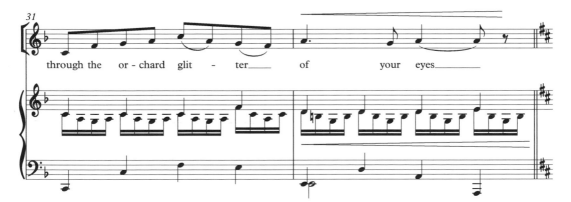

fin - ger-tips,____ Through the or-chard glit-ter of your eyes,____

through the or - chard glit - ter____ of your eyes____

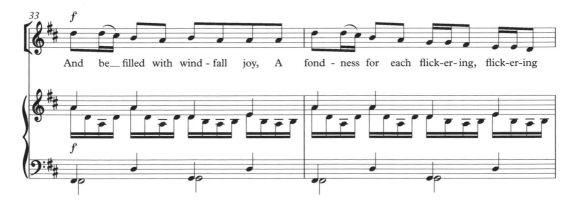

And be__ filled with wind-fall joy, A fond - ness for each flick-er-ing, flick-er-ing

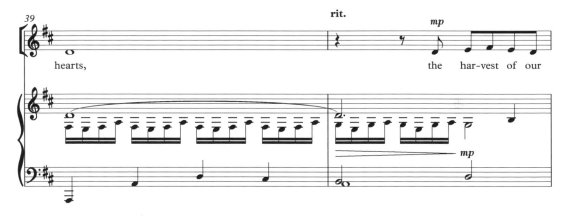

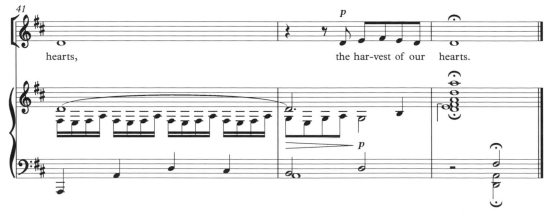

for Hans de Gilde, Barbara Comes, and the Ulmer Spatzen Chor

Night

Delphine Chalmers
(b. 1998)

BOB CHILCOTT
(b. 1955)

Duration: 2 mins

Make each snore a shib-bo-leth, Each mut-tered word a pro-mise To un-

Make each snore a shib-bo-leth, Each mut-tered word a pro-mise To un-

-lock the rich - es that are yours, To trust in the hope-ful heart___

-lock the rich - es that are yours, To trust in the hope-ful heart___

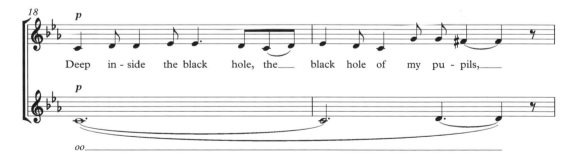

___ You___ car-ry as you jour - ney on.___

___ You___ car-ry as you jour - ney on.___

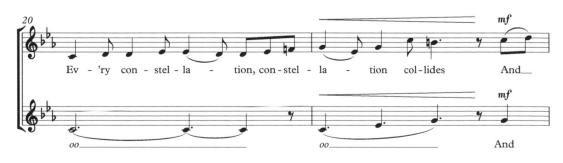

Deep in-side the black hole, the___ black hole of my pu-pils,___

oo___

Ev - 'ry con-stel-la - tion, con-stel-la - tion col-lides And___

oo___   oo___   And

for Hans de Gilde, Barbara Comes, and the Ulmer Spatzen Chor

Winter

Delphine Chalmers
(b. 1998)

BOB CHILCOTT
(b. 1955)

Duration: 3 mins

We've got our skates   on.

We   can't   see   for snow - drifts   But what do we care?

What do we care?   We've got our

unis.

skates   on.

mf sost.

We can't see for snow - drifts   But what do we care?

What do we care?   We've got our

skates   on.   We   can't   see   for   snow-

- drifts   But what do we care?

What do we care? We've got our skates on.

So, we'll

leave our foot-prints in the snow, foot-prints in the snow, we'll leave our foot-prints in the snow,

foot-prints in the snow. Our joy-ful words will hang in the crys - tal___ air, our

joy - ful words will hang in the crys - tal___ air As we re - vel in the

breath - less___ youth we___ share. We can't see for snow-

- drifts But what do we care?

What do we care? We've got our skates on.

We can't see for snow - drifts

But what do we care?   What do we care?

unis.

We've got our   skates on.

So, we'll snug-gle up be - fore the hearth,   be - fore the hearth,   we'll

snug-gle up be-fore the hearth, be-fore the hearth. With flames that spar - kle

in our eyes, with flames that spar - kle in our eyes, As we

wrap our friend-ship up in rib - bon ties.

We can't see for snow - drifts But what do we care?

What do we care?   We've got our

skates   on.   We   can't   see   for snow-

- drifts   But what do we care?

What do we care?   We've got our skates on.